I KNOW HIM

Catherine Johnson Broussard

I Am
thank you

ISBN 979-8-88751-338-6 (paperback)
ISBN 979-8-88751-339-3 (digital)

Christian Faith Publishing
832 Park Avenue
Meadville, PA 16335
www.christianfaithpublishing.com

Printed in the United States of America

I KNOW HIM
He sat on the stoop as I pass, this *Old Man*;
His eyes are on me.
I do not know *Him.*
He told me to "go home before the rain."
One drop of rain touches my face as I entered my door.
A storm is coming
Morning, the storm has passed.
A feeling of warmth surrounds me.
Still, I see this *Old Man* sitting on the stoop.
He told me to "go the other way to work."
I don't know why, but I listened.
No one is at work, a fire, blazing.
I pass the *Old Man* this evening.
His eyes are on me;
My eyes are on *Him*, *He* smiles,
I smile, and at that moment *I know who He is*!

As a child, skinny legged, belly never filled, eyes still closed, I remember playing happily, not knowing these days. I played in the wind, never questioning it, but it knew me. The wind shown me ways to go, ways which I never knew. The wind decided where to go without a care. Freedom. My imagination and my thoughts were with me, passing the time of day. Now, as an adult, much is known.

Things which were not clear then are now clear to me. My eyes were that of a child. I did not understand, yet I knew.

There are ten of us, but only eight chairs at the dinner table. I remember breakfast, not lunch. I do remember dinner and the large white plates placed in front of each chair and the water glasses neatly placed on the big wooden table. My childhood was something special, but it didn't seem that way as a child. Some things are still in my thoughts as if they just happened, but many are placed away. I remember Christmas, Thanksgiving, and the people visiting the house. The kinfolks were all shades of brown, hardworking, and proud people. They were loud, but loving. I would sit under the big wooden table with the clean white tablecloth and listen to the grown-ups tell their stories.

I remember the laughs of my brothers and sisters, the sounds of them running throughout the house as if they were in a big open field. I remember sitting on the cold wooden floor, seeing the earth between the wooden boards, passing the day with my thoughts. This I have done all my life. I was at peace knowing only what was around me. We often had family gathering; the kinfolks were in the front room talking and yelling. That's just the way they spoke to each other, no disrespect. I hear my brothers running and the screen door slamming. *I'm listening to the kinfolk trying to understand them, but I'm tired of these old folk talking. I can't even understand them no way,* thinking to myself.

I crawled from under the wooden table as the grown-ups yelled at me, "Get your butt from under that table, and go play outside." I moved as fast as I could because Ms. Lillie took off her shoe to swat my butt. I was happy playing outside and playing in the leaves as they fell to the ground. The leaves made a soft bed which I would jump and crawl around in. I love to watch the insects, but I do not like to touch them. The caterpillars ate their stomach full, but don't know the dangers around them. Their soft cloudlike blackness shines as their movement dances across the leaves not knowing that they are not safe. One strike, they are down, never to be remembered. I remember dancing in the rain as it fell. I remember my brothers and sisters laughing until our bellies ached. We played, laughed, and danced all day and night, with the thoughts of a child.

Morning! I like to wake with the sun. A new day, yet the same as the day before. "What will I do today?" I asked myself and said to myself, "Anything you want to!" I smiled. Breakfast is not ready so, I put on my clothes to go outside. As I looked at the houses on the block, the smell of the neighbors washing their porches was in the air; the smell was all too familiar. I see my mama sweeping the porch, all worries from the past days are washed away, all anew. My house is at 7444 Abundant Street. The house was big, old, light blue and sat in the middle of the block. There was a big tree in the front yard and bushes framed the walkway.

Two large green wooden chairs were placed in the center of the porch which wrapped around the house. A large picture window allowed the light to come in; It was our eyes to the world. "They are still here. When are the kinfolk gonna leave?" I said to myself. I still hear them in the house laughing and talking. I think that they will be leaving soon. I know this because they see mama sweeping, and they don't want the broom to touch their feet. I don't know why. Now I see them hopping as they leave the porch. "Don't let the broom touch your feet!" I screamed.

I see my friends playing down the street, and I started running as fast as my skinny legs would take me. "Watch out for those cars," mama yelled. "Yes, ma'am. The street is wide and uneven. The cars can just go around me," I said under my breath.

This is when I first saw *Him*, the *Old Man* with the same color as me, no worry in *His piercing eyes, eyes of fire,* yet they console me. *His* hair, white. *He* seems different, but peacefully different, grounded. *His hands* were strong with a touch of *grace,* but old, as if *He* has much work to do. *He* wore a night shirt, the kind they wore long, long, long time ago. I have not seen *Him* before, knowing that I would have remembered. *He* sat on the stoop of *His* large blue *house* which seems to have *many rooms.* Most of the houses in the neighborhood are blue, but *His* blue *house* looks and feels peacefully different. I don't know what kind of different, but just different, calming. *He* is just sitting there, wearing a *gold scarf* which wraps *His neck.* I knew that *He* was going to get warm since the sun seems to settle on *His face. He* does not have shoes on *His* burnished bronze *feet.*

My eyes are on *Him*, not wanting to turn away. *His eyes* are on me as if they found their place. *He* is not doing much, just sitting. I am still looking at Him and for a moment, with all authority, yet calmness, *He* said, "Stop." I listened as the car barely touched me. "He shields me," I said, not knowing why. I see Millie standing in the street. I ran over to her and asked, "Millie, can I ride your bike?"

"Yes, you can, but just go around the block."

"I will," I said and without hesitation, I jumped on the yellow bike with pink and white ribbon falling from each handlebar. I was riding as the wind greeted me, and I rode as fast as the bike could carry me. *I never had a bike, always wanted one.* "I should have put shoes on and maybe a jacket," I said to myself. I rode quickly down the street forgetting all, just being. "Maybe Millie would let me ride her bike to the park. It's only two blocks, not far at all."

Millie is watching me with a frown on her face. "Can I ride your bike to the park?" I asked with the joy of thinking that this was my bike. "No," she said. "I saw you running to my house and that car almost hit you."

"Okay, I promise to ride slow."

"You betta 'cause my mama will whoop me if you damage my bike." I quickly jumped on her bike before she changed her mind. "Okay, thank you," I yelled and again the wind took me to places which were only in my imagination. I passed the *Old Man* again as *He* sits on the stoop, knowing what just happened. *His eyes* are still on me.

"I wish that I had money to buy a snowball. All this riding has made me thirsty. I want a big red one, but it costs twenty cents. I wish that I had twenty cents. I never had twenty whole cents, but why should this day be any different?" I see my friends at the park, and they have snowballs. *Where did they get the twenty cents from? Their mamas must be rich. Maybe their daddies gave them the money. Their daddies must have good jobs.* I see Mattie sitting on the bench sipping her snowball, she spots me. "Hey, Mae, do you want some juice from my snowball?" Matti said in her sweet voice. "Hey, girl. You know I do." As I approached Mattie and her bright red snowball, I could feel the coolness of it. "Just a little slip. Don't drink all of the juice."

"Just a little more," I said. "Girl, I'm thirsty."

"Oh look, you got the cherry. That means another snowball."

"Yes, that's surely what it means," I said and without hesitation, I rode slowly to the snowball shop just up the street. I arrived holding the cherry like a precious jewel in my hand. I placed it gently on the counter. Miss Fancy, a fat-faced light-brown-skinned woman, looked at me and smiled. "You sure look like you want a snowball. What color do you want, baby?" Miss Fancy said with a wide smile showing her crooked teeth. "A red one, please."

"One large red snowball coming up."

As I waited, my mouth prepared itself for the sweetness of the snowball. "Here you go, baby." As Miss Fancy handed me the large red snowball, I bit into the sugary ice without stopping. "Slow down, baby. Your head is gonna ache."

"Thank you, ma'am," I said as I jumped on the bike. The coolness of the snowball settled in the pit of my mouth feeding all the places which sought its cool sugary juices. As a child, I am easily fulfilled. Riding still, the thought of breakfast came to mind. I know that my mama cooked grits, eggs, and smoked sausage with biscuits.

I know that she cooked a lot. She always does, and it is waiting for me. I know that my brothers and sisters are laughing, and daddy and mama are smiling. "Watch out for the rock in the road! As I tried to dodge the rock, I fell off the bike. *That stupid rock! I hope that I did not break anything. Millie will sure be mad.* I dust off my knees and check the bike. Thank God, the bike is not broken. Now, I don't remember what I was thinking about. Oh, breakfast, which is waiting for me, but my stomach feels full. I don't want anything. Did the sweet snowball fill me or was it the thought of breakfast which is waiting for me? Suddenly a settled feeling surrounds me. I see the *Old Man* smiling, still sitting on the stoop as I passed *Him*. A *red scarf* now covers *His neck*, a look of contentment is on *His face. He* watches me as I fade out of *His sight*. I see Millie. She looks mad. "I'm sorry," I said. "Here's your bike."

"You ain't gonna ride it no more. You took too long."

"Sorry," I said. "Are you still my friend?" I yelled as I ran home. As I entered my house, the smell of breakfast cooking was not there. Nothing was on the big table. I hear cries coming from the other room, my brothers and sisters are in there. Daddy is not here; Mama is gone too.

The taste of the sugary sweetness still fills my stomach. *I guess mama will come home soon. I know this* because *supper is later*. I sat in the large living room filled with old yet neat things. A large brown sofa sits under the large picture window, a comfortable green chair is in one corner, and a small blue chair is in the other next to a bookcase. A glass table is in the center of the room. While sitting on the sofa looking out of the window, I see the trees; their branches are praising the *Lord*. I see them in the clouds, the kinfolk from the old days. Their shapes pass by slowly, fading away as the white fluffy clouds change shapes. The house is settled, and my brothers and sister are playing. They don't know of my worries: their age has not come. I prepare oatmeal; our heads are bowed, and we eat.

After breakfast, I return to the sofa and continue to look out of the window. I see mama coming up the street, a brown bag in her hand, no, two bags, one in each hand. As she enters the house, a smile framed her face. Mama removes her coat and a *red scarf* from around her neck; a *red scarf* which I have not seen her wear before but which seems somewhat familiar. Mama places the bags gently on the table.

With her soft withered hands, she removes a pot from the cupboard and begins cooking. Mama removes one pot, then two pots and three pots, food-filled each pot. My mama is a small thin woman with long black hair which was given to her by her Choctaw grandmother. She have the walk of them, and the many worries on her shoulders are clear. Before the sun wakes, my mama's voice fills the house with song. Her voice, the softness, and the richness of it prepare us for the day. (singing) "Jesus, on the mainline, tell Him what you want," bellows out of her mouth. "Call *Him* up and tell *Him* what you want. If you are weak and can't get up, tell *Him* what you want, call *Him* up, and tell *Him* what you want." Mama's voice was our strength; as a child, I did not know this. I listen to mama's singing, the smell of the food, and the sounds of the white plates hitting the big wooden table calm my worries, if only for this time.

The day has passed, night falls, and our stomachs are full. Mama is in her closet again talking to herself; this is what a child knows. I sleep with two of my sisters in two small beds pushed together. One sister on one side and the other sister on the other side, me in the middle, protected. The coverings on our beds do not match, but warm my small frame. When I'm sleeping, I dream in color, bright blues, green, gold, and purples, never walking, always floating.

Morning, blessings for another day. I hear my brothers and sisters playing outside. I see the clouds; they look sad, and the sun is afraid to come out. I look down the street. I see the *Old Man*, sitting on the stoop, looking at the sky. *He is* just looking, *lips* moving slightly. Somehow *His presence* is needed. "Mae, come outside!" my sister yells as she sees me looking out of the window. I rushed to put my clothes and shoes on and run outside to play. "Catch the ball," my brother said. "Okay, brother, but don't throw it hard."

"Just catch the ball, stupid, if you want to play." My brothers, all seven of them, are skinny, tall, and never wearing shoes. They were born three years apart with me and my sisters in the middle. We all have dirty red/orange hair, and skin all different shades of brown. Our eyes are light to dark brown; history is shown in us.

I hear thunder; it roars slightly. I look at the clouds again. They are still angry; they're gray and black clouds now. The wind blows as if it was in a rush. Leaves are scattered everywhere. "Let's play in the leaves," my brother said as his skinny long legs moved throughout the leaves. In a moment, there is stillness, the *Old Man is standing, His voice came out of the wind as if He was made of it. HE whispers,* demanding, yet purposely, "Seek your mother." *As He stood, I could see His very essence, His* brightness forced my eyes to close. Within seconds, my mama stood in the doorway telling us to come inside. The smell of rain became stronger. One drop of rain hit my face as I entered the door. My oldest sister closed the windows and curtains. I see the lighting in the sky as it filled the room, thunder followed. A storm is here, yet later that night, I rest securely, without hesitation.

In the morning, the storm has passed, a feeling of warmth surrounds me. Daddy is not home. Mama is in the kitchen cooking. Same house, different feeling. Mama's singing fills the kitchen; sadness is in her voice. "Ya'll children go out and play. Breakfast is almost ready." We all rushed to put on our clothes and shoes and hurried to see what the storm has brought. All the rain has passed, and the sun is smiling again, yet the storm is still here. "Where is daddy?" my little sister asked. "Gone to work I think." Her fat face smiled at me as she began to play. *The sky is peaceful, but why was she so angry yesterday?* "Breakfast!" my mama yelled out of the window. "You children, come on inside and eat."

Plates of eggs and grits decorated the big wooden table, water in each glass. All heads are bowed as mama's trembling yet stern voice began to bless the food. I see worry in her eyes; she hurts. "*Lord,* thank *You* for protecting us last night and the nights to come. A storm that *You* sent passed over us. I lay down and woke up in safety, for *You* were watching over us. *Lord,* continue to keep us. I know that *You* will. Have mercy on those whose eyes and ears are closed to *Your Word.* We know that *You* are in control. We thank *You,* knowing that *You* are never far away. In Jesus's name, we pray. Amen and Amen."

"Mama, where is the butter?" I asked. "Child, eat your breakfast, hurry. We have to go to church." We all ate, some at the table and others sitting on the floor. Our bellies are full. Mama's cooking was skillfully learned, from her mother, then her mother, and then her mother. Much pride was taken, and much was made from so little. After breakfast, we all took our baths, water only changing twice. The little ones first, then the older children; mama was always last. My big sisters combed the girls' hair, and the boys' hair was brushed quickly before they started squiring. We had on our Sunday's clothes; my brothers with shined shoes from the night before, and we girls had ribbon in our hair.

We quickly walked to the church, which was not far, only seven blocks. We passed many neighbors on the way to the church. Mama always told us if we saw the whites of someone's eyes as we passed them, we should always greet them. Also, if we didn't speak, the old people would tell mama, and you know what was going to happen.

As I said my morning hellos to the people as they passed, I saw the *Old Man* sitting on the stoop, smiling as *He* was looking up to the heavens. *He* was talking, but I did not see anyone around *Him. His eyes* have no worries. They always seem fulfilled. *His eyes* were on me. *He smiled* at me and whispered in my ear, never leaving the stoop, "*I Am* here." The *Old Man* has a copper basket in *His hand*, which is full of leaves, the same leaves I see perfectly placed around *His house*. The neighborhood is in disarray due to the storm yesterday. Many are outside cleaning up and removing leaves and branches. I glanced at my house; all is settled, nothing out of place. *The Old Man's house* is perfect; a ray of light covers *His house*. I hear music coming from *His house*, the kind of music which comes to ease all. I look up at my mama; she smiles at me as she pass the *Old Man's house*. I feel peace which I am yet to understand.

The old ones say that the church has stood for many years, about 150 to this date. It has been well kept, but the pews are old, yet comfortable; they are worn in like an old glove. We took our seats and quickly began singing. Church is always a happy place for me, my brothers and sisters. My mama's face now seems hopeful. Joyful singing fills the church. The people are jumping, and sometimes they run around, and no one tells them to stop. Of course, my brothers run around the church each time someone runs. They don't know why they are running and neither do I; all we know is that it is fun to see.

One Sunday I asked Sister Ruth, "Why do the people run?" She told me that "they are filled with the Holy Ghost." So that is why I don't run; a child's mind doesn't understand. Pastor Sir, his given name is Sir Morgan, is a tall dark-skinned man who is always neatly dressed. He has five children, and they all sit on the first pew with his wife Sister Nedra. Sister Nedra is a brown-skinned, small-framed woman, who is very nice. Pastor Sir has a strong voice which seems to muster up all the old ones from long ago. To begin the service, Pastor would always shout, "Good morning, church!" as he greets all. With the great response, the church would say, "Good morning, Pastor." I listened to the pastor as a child, not knowing much, just an empty vessel waiting to be filled. Before the sermon, Pastor Sir always voiced, "Only what you do for Christ will last." As a child, I do not understand; it is not clear to me yet.

I know all the people in the church. I see them in the neighborhood and play with their children. Some of the neighbors are delightful. They would bring food to my mama because they say that "there are too many children in that house." Others are just nosey. Mama always knew the nosey ones; she should begin to pray and within seconds they would flee. The neighbors brought clothes and other stuff too; my mama is always grateful.

He is here, the Old Man. I searched the church even standing up to look for *Him. I do not see Him, but I know that He is here. His eyes are watching me. Where is He?* I stood up again, but my mama looked at me with those eyes, and I quickly sat down.

The praying, praising, and singing have not stopped. Three hours have passed, and I am still sitting in the same pew. A church fan is in everyone's hand, and the feet stomping continues. "Today we have a special offering," Pastor Sir said. "Dig deep in your pocket, your purses. One of our church members is in need." Mama always gave us a nickel for the offering. I often thought about keeping my nickel, but my hands won't allow me to do so; my feet always lead me to the offering table.

Now it's time for the offering. I began slowly walking to the offering table, swaying back and forth and singing, "I will trust in the *Lord*. I will trust in the *Lord* until I die." I feel *His presence*. I know that the *Old Man* is watching me. *I'm looking around the church, but I do not see Him.*

"Stop looking around," old Miss Scott said. Miss Scott is old as dirt; she wears this stinky perfume, always stinking up the church. "Yes, ma'am," I said with a frown on my face. I placed my nickel on the offering plate. *As I looked at the plate, I see leaves, the same leaves from the Old Man's copper basket.* I am comforted; solace surrounds me. This is the same feeling I felt many times before. I want to stay in *it*. I returned to my pew, and I told my mama about the leaves; she smiled and looked at me with a look of knowing.

After much more preaching, singing, and shouting, the church service is about to end. With his strong voice, Pastor Sir asked mama to come to the front of the church. We all stood, worried. My brothers, sisters, and I started praying because we knew that our brothers did something bad. My brothers began to cry, and all were saying that they were sorry and will not do it again. My mama looked at them with that stern motherly look and walked to the altar as the pastor requested. I don't know what my brothers were confessing, but it was not about them. A special offering was given to my mama. I received five nickels that day.

Ten years have passed; breakfast, lunch, and dinner each day. Daddy is not at home.

I am older; eyes are open more than before. It's the ending of high school, a new chapter. All my friends are walking to school; it is nice to see them; they all are older. I ran to catch up to them. "Girl, ready for school?" Ruth said. "Yes, our last year in high school. Can you believe it?"

"That's a cute dress. I love your shoes. Now you think that you are grown? No, but I am looking forward to this school year. Do you have any plans?"

"Yes," I told Ruth, "I'm thinking about college, Spellman or maybe Howard."

"You have good grades. I know that you would get in either one." As I listen to Ruth, *I see His house. Yes! I knew that He would be there, the Old Man; He is sitting on the stoop and is smiling at me. I smile back at Him.* I'm a little wiser than the days before. Life has a way of getting you to see things differently. Yet I do not understand the peace I feel when I see the *Old Man. I continue to watch Him, not wanting to turn away.*

"Who is that?" Ruth said with fear in her voice. Still looking at the *Old Man as He stands,* "Who is that? Who is that in the car?" Ruth screamed, "Mae! Watch out, the man in the car!" As I turned away from the *Old Man*, to look at Ruth, a large hand grabs my arm. The man in the car, his eyes are big and red; a crocked smile covers his face. Hitting and biting his arm does not stop him. As I turn to look to my friends for help, the *Old Man was by my side. He whispered,* "Trust in me." *I was not shaken.* I was in *perfect peace*, and at that moment, I was safe in the *Old Man's arms.* The man in the car is behind us.

Schooling begins, a new school. The same children are in my class; it has been that way since the second grade. Tilly is not here; she was my best friend from the second to fifth grades. One morning while Tilly was walking to the store, she disappeared; someone took her. The old people say that they took her because she was so pretty. Many looked for her, but she was not found. The authority searched also which was surprising, but still, they could not find her. Tilly was only ten years old.

I remember playing in the park with her. She was a quiet, shy child, not wanting much. At times, I think I see Tilly still, playing in the park and swinging on the swings. I know it's not her, but the girl always smiles at me when she sees me. She also wears the same purple dress that Tilly wore on Sundays to church.

I remember Michael Boss who also left us. Michael was a dark-skinned boy who always wanted to be first—first in line, knowing that he had to be last in line because he was taller than the other boys. Michael was a happy child, not wanting to get into trouble, a humble boy. He was the teacher's pet. Each Friday he would bring flowers to our teacher from his mother's garden just to get a kiss on his cheek.

One Friday evening, Michael was playing near the False River throwing rocks into the water. The river was at the back of town; we were told not to go there. Two boys from another neighborhood, one with no front teeth because they were knocked out during a fight and the other boy who was big for his age, started throwing rocks at Michael. They hit him several times in his head, and he fell to the ground never getting up again. Michael died four days later. The two boys were arrested and are still in the old jailhouse. What a waste of life.

The old people say that Michael is buried under the big pecan tree. The big tree sits in the middle of the yard of Michael's house. I believe this is said only because pecans were found in Michael's pockets. I pass the tree each morning and evening to and from school. I don't know much about the growth of trees, but this tree is always in bloom. The neighbors call it the Happy Tree or Michael's Tree because it drops pecans all year long.

On the way home, from school, I walk with my friends, and we gather pecans which fell from Michael's tree. We always ate them on our way home. "We have pecans all year long," Beth said. As I listened to her, I thought, *How is this possible? Why is this tree out of all the other trees in full bloom all year long?* I see *Him,* the *Old Man.* I look closely at *Him* because my eyes won't let me see differently. *His* calmness steadies my feet.

As I pass by Michael's tree, *the Old Man is watching me. I am watching Him. Is that Michael running and playing under the pecan tree?* I call out his name, "Michael!" with excitement in my voice, but he doesn't answer. Does he hear me?

"Why are you calling for Michael?" Beth said, "You know that he is in heaven." But I can see Michael clearly under the tree. He is playing, and the *Old Man* is standing near him. But the *Old Man's eyes* are on me. "Mae, what are you looking at?" Beth said.

"Do you see the *Old Man,* and do you see Michael playing under the tree?"

"Girl, stop playing. There is no one under the tree."

"Let's skip home." I grabbed Beth's arm, and we began skipping home. *The Old Man is still watching me, and Michael is still playing under the big pecan tree.*

Saturday morning, Sunday comes early. I wake with the sun; it shines on my face. Anxiously, I put on my clothes and shoes and hurried back to Michael's tree looking for the *Old Man* and Michael. I look everywhere; the *Old Man* is not here nor is Michael. Looking at the pecan tree, I see that it is in full bloom, "How is that so? I know that everything has its season." *Around the corner is the Old Man's* house. *I will see if they are there.*

I walk the block to see if the *Old Man* is sitting on the stoop. As I look at the house, a feeling of peacefulness overwhelms me. I see the beautiful trees in full bloom, and the flowers in the garden are adorned with the most amazing colors. The birds are singing; peace surrounds me. *Is the Old Man inside? Should I look in the window?* As I step on the grass, there is a need to remove my shoes, so I remove them.

With each step, my feet are placed gently on the soft green grass. The sun beams on me. I just want to sing and dance! *The sun and birds are different. The birds are singing.* "What kind of birds are in the trees?" *Each bird has its own color, one more amazing than the other, the colors of my dreams. I see Michael's tree in the backyard. I never noticed this before. Should I look inside?* A feeling of pure protection surrounds me. Everything is in its place. I looked at the house again. *Should I look inside? No, it is not my time to see. I am not ready.* As I turn away, I see the *Old Man* sitting on the stoop. *His eyes are watching me.*

Now, ten years have passed, and many things have happened over the years. I achieved my biggest dream; I finished my schooling at the university. The years at the university have brought wisdom and an awakening, a source of peace and strength. As I arrive closer to home, the peace I felt as a child surrounds me.

Most of the neighbors are still here, but many have gone to their glory. However, I know that the old ones would be proud of me. As a child, going to college was always my hope. Achieving my degree is an accomplishment; however I had many battles to fight. Role models were few as well as opportunities.

I remember in the eleventh grade, a new history teacher arrived at the school. His name was Mr. Russ Cornel. Mr. Cornel was a tall, light-skinned black man who wore a brown suit each day, only the shirt and ties changed. He spoke with roughness in his voice, but his words were encouraging. He talked about the past, telling us to never forget the struggle of our families. Mr. Cornell explained that knowing our past and the struggles of the people will give us a better understanding of who we are.

One Thursday after school, Mr. Cornell asked me to stay; he wanted to talk to me. He talked about his days at the university and how proud he was that he had the opportunity to attend. He said that being at the university gave him a sense of placement and feeding the mind of the young ones was his mission. As I listened, I could see the strength in his shoulders, the boldness they present, the pride in his walk, and the way he held his head high. His voice was strong with no words of uncertainty. He spoke as if the old ones were in the room with him. His eyes were without fear striking my soul. He spoke about the *Lord* and how he prayed for guidance. It was then that I knew I needed what he had.

Finally, home. All seems small; the houses are the same, but their years are showing. As I turned the corner, I see it—*His house*, and *He* is sitting on the stoop as if *He* knew of my arrival. The *Old Man* is the same as I remembered, looking at me. I look at *Him* through the car window. *He* is watching me. I am without question.

I see my house, 7444 Abundant Street; it looks the same, yet a little smaller. Mama is sitting on the old green rocking chair on the porch; she smiles as I step out of the car. Her face shows tiredness, but proudness emits in the corner of her eyes. "I see you," she said. I ran to her and nestled my head in her bosom only to feel a mother's touch. I said, "I see you, mama." My two sisters are at home with mama. Daddy has not been there since way back when. The house smells the same—the same sofa, chair, and big wooden table. But new knowledge is in the house. I look again at my mama; her face shows grace with a faint hint of contentment. You see, none of my brothers nor sisters have seen the inside of a jailhouse. All are in good health with a mission in life. Our foundation is planted firmly.

My oldest brother, the one who was always running, managed to run straight to the church where he preaches each Sunday. He preaches at the same church we went to as children. Mama and them sit on the first pew each Sunday. Mama says that the *Lord* has smiled upon all twelve of her children. My oldest sister and the sister next to her are at home taking care of mama. I often wonder if they wanted a different life.

As I continue to the living room, my oldest sister sits on the sofa looking through the window. Knowing that I entered the room, she said in her soft voice, "You finally finished college. You have been there for a lifetime." I smiled and hugged her; the smell of lilies filled our space. "Yes, I did," I said, and she smiled at me. Her eyes showed warmth with a touch of sadness. She looks smaller, her spirit has tapered; life has its way. That is why it's good not to always be settled. Your spirit must be free, free to grow, free to create, free to be.

My sister is proud of me; this I know, but sadness is in her heart, still. Maybe she believes that my life was easy, not knowing of my hardships. I often think about my accomplishments. I know that I finished college because I have the paper to prove it, but all my paths must have been straightened. I had many trials.

I remember my first week in college, the first day of class; I was told that I was not approved for financial assistance. The counselor at my high school worked with me in completing my application, so I was unsure what happened. I had a choice that day to go to class or not. I remember talking to myself as I did as a child. I see now that it was not myself I was speaking with. Somehow, I found my way. I knew that I had to go to class.

As I walked into the large classroom only one chair was left, chair number 444. I sat in the chair, and my schooling began. Later that day, I was informed of the mix up in the Financial Aid office and that my tuition along with a payment for my books were approved. My lunch for the year was paid for along with $888 to spare. A few months later, I was informed that my tuition was paid for my entire stay at the university. Funds were donated by a wealthy man to assist some students who were in need. I do not know how I become one of the students. As for the donor, I only know that *He* is a wealthy man, the only son of someone who is the creator of the university.

During my second year, after taking an English class, I was offered a seat in a much sought-out literature class. This offer was based upon my poetry submission, an assignment from my English class. I do not call myself a poet. I am connected to words as if they are speaking to me, and I am listening. Words and the expression of words were always with me. My thoughts are real to me, words spoken from that place in my soul. However, the poem which I submitted was chosen, and I was told that I was a poet.

Once I became settled at the university and during my second year, I would wander around the campus, one with myself. I remember the river behind the university; the students were told not to walk along the river, but the land was calling me. Large oak trees were everywhere, and the sound of birds singing reminds me of home. I walked peacefully through the trees and the tall grass; I was in that place, *overwhelming peace.*

This Saturday while walking along the river, I knew that the *Old Man* was there. I am comforted. Singing fills my walk. A few feet away, I see a cabin which is covered in vines; it's a small wooden cabin with one door and three broken windows. Scattered on the ground are wildflowers beautiful in color. They led me to a pathway to the torn-down porch. Looking through the window, the presence of hardship is clear. "I want to go in, but I don't want to move. I need to see more, but the feeling of sorrow is overwhelming." My feet take me to the porch, over leaves and rocks I am at the front door. My hands push the door open; I fall to my knees. My eyes are close.

I see her, this thin dark-brown-skinned woman with a strong frame; she is cooking by the fireplace. There are two children, a girl and a boy. The girl seems about ten years and the boy about seven. They are sitting on the floor near the fireplace in the back of the cabin. The thin woman is singing a song I do not know, but my soul knew. I listen as she sings and watch the children's faces. Their faces are the same as mine as a child. The children are smiling, but their eyes are sad.

As I look around the cabin, I see a large wooden table like the table at my house. There are four chairs. A large kettle is placed in the middle of the table. Still singing, I watch the woman take food from the kettle and prepare each plate. I look again at the woman; sadness covers her face. Her hands shake as she places the plates on the table. The girl and boy hurry to the table and gently bow their heads. The same prayer my mama said, and her mother said was spoken by the woman. "*Lord*, keep us. I know that You will. I know that You are in control and are never far away. Have mercy on those whose eyes and ears are close to Your Words. Knowing that You will never leave us, in Jesus's name, we pray. Amen and Amen."

Do they see me. I don't think so. Why are they here? In a child's voice, the little boy looks at his mother and said, "Mama, I know that we will be all right."

The mother smiled and asked, "How do you know child?"

With fullness in his voice, the young boy said, "The *Old Man* told me."

"What *Old Man*? the mother asked.

"The *Old Man* who sits on the stoop of the big *blue house* at the end of the road. He told me that, 'Weeping is for a night, but joy comes in the morning.' That's what He told me, mama." The woman wept. Peace settled in the child's eyes. *He is here, the Old Man. I know that He is watching me. He is watching them.*

On the way back to the university, I continue to think about the woman and her children. *Why were they there? Should I tell someone?* After walking for an hour, the first person that I see upon arrival on the campus is Mr. Will. Mr. Arthur Will is a history professor and is always here. We all look up to him; he has that way. Mr. Wills would tell the students, "Do not abandon the works of your hands." A child's mind does not yet understand.

Mr. Will wore a blue suit and worn-out boots. You can hear him coming down the hall because the heels on his boots are made from copper. I guess that was needed to carry his strong study feet. "Mr. Will, may I speak to you?" I asked.

"Yes, but make it quick. I have work to do." I told Mr. Will, about walking along the river, and before I could finish, he said, "Child, didn't they tell you not to go back there?"

"Yes, sir, but I—"

"But nothing. I know it was calling you, but you must learn to listen and be still."

"Yes, sir, but I needed to go," I said.

"Yes, I understand, I do know that *He* will protect *His* faithful ones."

With all my attention toward *him* as His voice commanded, Mr. Will said, "I want you to read something." He was speaking about a paper he wrote. Arriving at Mr. Will's office, he handed me his paper. The papers were written a long time ago as the papers were worn and stained. However, the way in which he handed the papers to me was as if they were his life's work. I told Mr. Will, "Thank you," and hurried to my room. After completing my chores and after talking to myself in the closet, I settled down and began reading.

"I know that we are one, one with the Creator. His eyes are watching us." The first words struck me as if I knew all of what he was saying. The papers continue with "*He* was there at the beginning of all which is. He is with the old ones, with all, telling His secrets. The old ones knew, I now know Him. The old ones sought Him, they listened. He is in their stride, their talk, their weaknesses, their strengths; all the time revealing His glorious mercy. As a father knows each of his children, He knows our voices and every thought, telling us that we are not perfect, but we are His children. He will reveal to some His ways, but you must not lean on your own understanding. Allow Him to direct your path."

Today my eyes are seeing and hearing not as a child. Hearing these words is new, yet familiar to me, not in speech, but in the *Old Man's eyes.* Mr. Will's papers revealed much to me, growth. The next day I returned his papers and thanked him. In a profound voice, he responded, "No, thank Him. He knows who you are and all that you are to be. He is speaking to you. He will always lead you to your purpose, be still and listen. Mae Johnson, you must know that the peace you feel is your validation." I see Mr. Will. He seems different. I don't know what kind of different, but peacefully different. *He* is watching me as I walk away; *His* eyes are on me.

I surely miss mama's cooking. Greens with pickled meat, rice and cornbread, one of my favorite meals. I know that the meal will be waiting for me. My mama has a way of knowing; she hears *Him*; she listens for *Him*. After supper, we all gathered around and spoke about the years. Seeing today, all is different, yet the same. Mama's years are showing, the same as my brothers and sisters. No one talks about daddy. I am unclear why he left; I guess life has its way. I have not seen him since I was a child, never saying goodbye, only remembering that he said, "I will see you kids when I come home." He smiled and walked away caring his toolbox in one hand and a cup of coffee in the other.

I remember my dad; I remember his hands; they were big and strong. My dad is a carpenter, and with one strike of the hammer, the nail would drive completely into the wood. I don't know where he is now; the kinfolk say that he is in Mississippi. This may not be true since I see him riding the bus or walking down the street. I call to him, but he doesn't answer. I cannot ask mama where daddy is. I don't like to see the look on her face.

I spoke to my sister today as she was sketching. I asked her, "Why didn't you leave?" My sister told me, "Baby, all that I need is right here." As she spoke, I looked at what she was sketching; it was a picture of the *Old Man's house*. Of course, I know *His house*; it is settled in me. *His House* was perfectly drawn as light seems to radiate from the paper. I didn't know that my sister was an artist. I see my sister; she is searching for something; maybe she found it which is why she did not leave. Her hands are steady as she draws the sun as it comes to rest upon the *Old Man's face* as it always did.

The sun seems to know its place. "I am comforted, little sister. I have a need to stay here with mama and them," she said. "I don't know why, but I am needed here." My sister spoke about the time she was walking home, and two men attacked her. "Sis, I was walking home, one with myself, peace surrounds me. As I got closer to home, two large men, both with unrecognizable faces, jumped from the bushes. One tried to grab me, but I did not feel his strength, and the other man was behind me and fell to his knees. The *Old Man* who sat on the stoop was there with open arms. My feet directed me to *Him*. The two men were behind *Him*. I was out of their reach. Maybe I was dreaming, but I don't think so. The peace I felt that night is with me still." That evening, my sister and I spoke for hours, I listened to all she had to say. Now I know why she did not leave.

In the morning, I wake with the sun, smiling, still. During breakfast, I hear joyful sounds coming from each pot; Mama is cooking. There are twelve chairs at the big wooden table, white plates placed neatly in front of each chair, and water glasses beside them. We all sit, bow our heads, and mama blesses the food, not one word out of place.

After breakfast, I gathered myself to go outside. Looking around the neighborhood, a sense of joy fills me; I see Millie and her children. They are riding their bikes as we did as children. "Hi, Mae," she yelled, "I am happy that you are home. We will talk later. "Okay", I yelled.

Without a thought, I look down the street to *His house*. My soul seeks *Him. He* is there as I knew *He* would be, the *Old Man*, sitting on the stoop waiting for me. I walk slowly to *His house*; my feet take me, knowing the way. *His eyes are on me. Should I speak to Him? Looking at Him, I hear His voice. Speaking to me as if He knows me. His voice, a familiar voice. The same voice I heard as a child, the same voice I heard as the car barely touched me. The same voice which protected me from the men in the car, the same voice that was with me in the church and at the university, the same voice I heard near the river, the voice that I hear today. I looked at the Old Man again as He sat on the stoop. His eyes are on me, my eyes are on Him, He smiles, I smile, and at that moment I know who He is!*

About the Author

Catherine Johnson Broussard is an African American poet, author, and activist living in New Orleans, Louisiana. "I always had a need to write. As a child, I remember writing my thought on pieces of paper knowing that someday I will share my words." Mrs. Broussard's first work of poetry was published in 1982; thereafter her poems have appeared in several books and publications. Mrs. Broussard's first book of poetry titled *His Words*, a book of inspirational poems, was published in 2019. She has a master's degree in social work from Southern University in New Orleans and is the owner of the Wedding Broom Company of New Orleans and the Freedom Key NOLA. Mrs. Broussard is a member of the Martin Luther King Jr. Exhibition Council and the National Conference of Artists, New Orleans Chapter.